I0693685

L.K. THURSTON

A Walk in the Woods

5 Ways to Appreciate Mother Nature, Regain Inner Peace, and Reconnect with the Earth to Replenish Your Soul

Copyright © 2024 by L.K. Thurston

All rights reserved. No part of this publication may be reproduced, stored or transmitted in any form or by any means, electronic, mechanical, photocopying, recording, scanning, or otherwise without written permission from the publisher. It is illegal to copy this book, post it to a website, or distribute it by any other means without permission.

L.K. Thurston asserts the moral right to be identified as the author of this work.

L.K. Thurston has no responsibility for the persistence or accuracy of URLs for external or third-party Internet Websites referred to in this publication and does not guarantee that any content on such Websites is, or will remain, accurate or appropriate.

Designations used by companies to distinguish their products are often claimed as trademarks. All brand names and product names used in this book and on its cover are trade names, service marks, trademarks and registered trademarks of their respective owners. The publishers and the book are not associated with any product or vendor mentioned in this book. None of the companies referenced within the book have endorsed the book.

First edition

This book was professionally typeset on Reedsy.
Find out more at reedsy.com

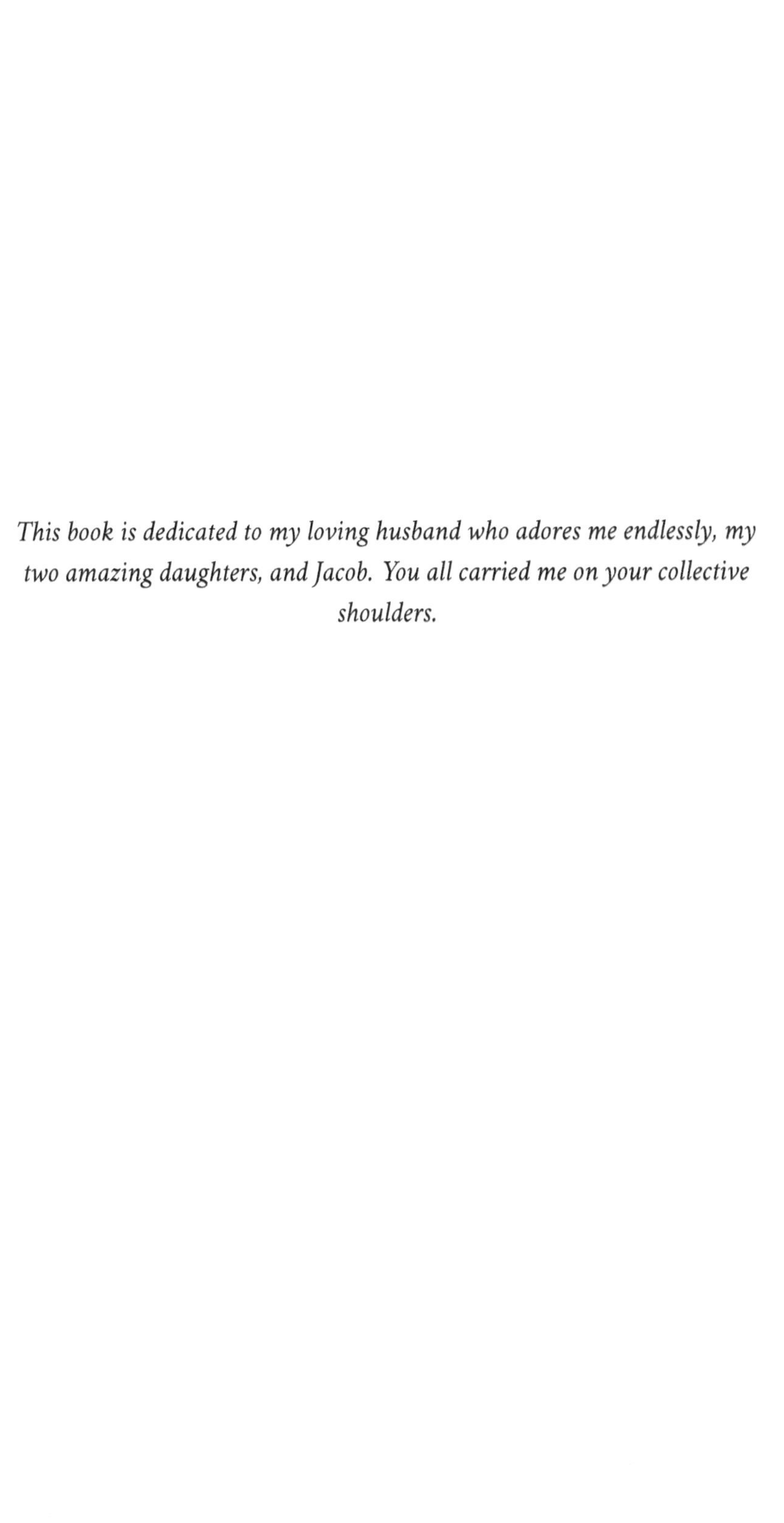

This book is dedicated to my loving husband who adores me endlessly, my two amazing daughters, and Jacob. You all carried me on your collective shoulders.

Contents

One

Introduction

Imagine standing at the edge of a dense forest. The towering trees sway gently with the breeze, their leaves creating a shimmering canopy that filters soft sunlight to the forest floor. The air smells of damp earth and pine, and you hear the faint rustle of unseen creatures moving in the underbrush. For a moment, you feel a quiet clarity, a grounding sense that you are part of something ancient, vast, and alive. In that fleeting moment, your thoughts quiet, your breath deepens, and you feel at peace. That moment—simple yet profound—is what this book is all about.

Welcome to *A Walk in the Woods: 5 Ways to Appreciate Mother Nature, Regain Inner Peace, and Reconnect with the Earth to Replenish Your Soul*. This book is an invitation to pause, step away from the noise of daily life, and rediscover your senses in the embrace of nature. Whether you are overworked, processing past traumas, or simply curious about connecting more deeply with the world around you, this book offers a path back to yourself through the natural world.

Why I Wrote This Book

As someone who has often felt the weight of modern life, I know what it means to feel disconnected—from yourself, from others, and from the earth beneath your feet. Like many, I spent years moving through life distracted, tethered to screens and schedules, feeling as though something essential was slipping away. Also, like many, I have experienced traumas, sadness, and overwhelm in my life. Then, one day in my late 30s after I sent my daughters off to college, my husband and I decided to buy a home in the middle of a 40-acre forested property in a very rural area. The nearest neighbor was a mile away, the nearest store a 45-minute drive, and internet services were patchy at best. Everyone said we were crazy, but something in me told me it was very right. What began as a spontaneous life decision, turned into a journey of healing and self-discovery.

With every adventure into new depths of my property, I not only discovered new flora and fauna, but that I began to feel a way I had not felt before. I felt awakened, lifted, opened, clear, and new. Walking through the woods, I realized how much I had been missing. The vibrant greens, the earthy scents, the intricate songs of birds—they awakened something within me. Each step reminded me that nature has the power to ground us, to heal us, and to reconnect us with what truly matters. I wrote this book to share what I have learned, so that you, too, might experience the transformative power of nature.

What This Short Book Will Teach You

This book is structured around a simple yet profound idea: reconnecting with nature through your five senses. Each chapter focuses on a different sense and offers practical, approachable ways to engage with the natural world. You do not need to be an experienced hiker or an avid outdoors person to benefit from this book. All you need is a willingness to slow down and let nature meet you where you are. I do recommend carrying a small notebook or journal so you may record your discoveries, your feelings, create small sketches, or capture any breakthroughs you may have on your journeys.

Here is a glimpse of what you will discover within these pages:

- **Seeing the Forest for the Trees:** How to truly observe the natural world through your sense of sight and really open your eyes to notice the intricate beauty that often veiled behind the rush of daily life.
- **Stop to Smell the Redwood:** How to unlock the healing potential of scents in nature, from the aroma of wildflowers to the crisp air after a rainstorm.
- **Do You Hear That?:** How to take out the earbuds and tune into the symphony of sounds in the wilderness, using them to quiet your mind and find inner stillness.
- **Feel the Elements:** How to reconnect to nature with the sense of touch, experiencing the textures and sensations of nature to ground yourself in the present moment.
- **Taste With Caution!:** How to safely explore the flavors of the natural world, and learn to appreciate its bounty with mindfulness and care.

Each chapter is filled with insights, and actionable tips designed to help you make the most of your time outdoors. You will learn how to use your senses as tools to anchor yourself in the moment, calm your anxieties, and replenish your soul.

How This Book Will Benefit You

The benefits of connecting with nature are both immediate and long-lasting. Scientific studies have shown that spending time in natural settings can reduce stress, improve mental clarity, and even enhance physical health. But beyond the science, there is something deeply personal and transformative about rediscovering your place in the world. As for myself, I was able to let go of past traumas that I clung to, find the strength to set boundaries for myself, build an open mind to create new channels of creativity and job opportunities, and find that I could attain overall happiness in this lifetime - all by allowing myself the time to become a part of the elements of the earth that is right outside my door.

By the end of this book, you will not only have practical techniques for immersing yourself in nature but also a renewed sense of wonder and belonging. You will feel more grounded, more present, and more connected to both the earth and yourself. Whether you are seeking a moment of calm in a hectic life or a deeper journey of self-discovery, this book will guide you.

The Journey Ahead

As we embark on this journey together, I encourage you to approach these pages with an open heart and a curious spirit. This is not just a book to read—it is a call to action. Step outside. Feel the sun on your skin, hear the crunch of leaves underfoot, and let the world remind you of its beauty and your place within it.

In the next chapter, we will begin with the sense of sight. Together, we will explore how to truly see the forest for the trees, noticing the details that bring the natural world to life. But for now, take a deep breath. Let the promise of this journey settle over you like a soft breeze. The woods are waiting, and so is the part of you that longs to reconnect.

Let us take that first step together.

Two

Seeing the Forest for the Trees

Close your eyes for a moment and imagine the forest. Picture the rich hues of green, the play of light and shadow, and the intricate patterns that seem to exist everywhere—in the bark of trees, in the veins of leaves, and in the shape of wildflowers. Sight is perhaps the most immediate sense we use to engage with the natural world, but it's also the one we often take for granted. In this chapter, we'll slow down and explore the forest through a fresh lens, learning to truly see—not just look—at the world around us.

Bugs

Starting below ground level, scaling up into the canopy of the forest, focus on the insects that make the forest their home. Look closely at the iridescent wings of a dragonfly as it flits across a stream to capture its prey. Watch as a spider creates the delicate architecture of its web, and how it sparkles with morning dew. Notice the patterns on a beetle's shell and how it moves the soil from the earth. Observe the purposeful movements of an ant carrying a burden many times its size, and how the colony works together to complete a task.

Bugs might seem insignificant, but from the microscopic gnat to the majestically large Luna Moth, they all play a pivotal role in this enormous ecosystem. Their diversity can be astonishing if you take the time to observe. Bring your eyes down to the level of the forest floor, where the smallest creatures reveal an extraordinary world.

Ground Plants and Rocks

Shift your gaze downward to the plants and rocks that blanket the forest floor. Mosses and lichens create intricate carpets in shades of green, gray, reds, and yellows. Tiny flowers, often overlooked, bloom in vibrant colors, their petals revealing hues irresistible to specific wildlife to propagate in another place in the forest.

Take note of the texture of rocks: some with jagged edges, others with smooth surfaces, or cracks filled with life—ferns, mushrooms, and other small wonders, even miniature ecosystems! Each rock and plant tell a story of the environment, from the moisture levels to the minerals present in the soil. Be sure to leave these seemingly barren features as you found them, as these are home fixtures to wildlife, and disrupting these habitats essentially disrupts their home. By doing this, harm may come to whatever may dwell here.

Forest Water Features

Streams, rivers, ponds, and even puddles add dynamic elements to the forest. Observe how water reflects the surrounding trees, sky, and sunlight, creating an ever-changing mirror. Watch the ripples caused by a leaf drifting downstream or a frog leaping into the water, and try to solve the mystery of how water striders can stay on top of the water's surface.

If you are near a waterfall, take in the contrast of its powerful motion against the stillness of the surrounding forest. Water features not only enhance the forest visually but also invite you to pause and reflect, drawing your gaze into their rhythmic movements.

Common Forest Mammals

While mammals are often harder to spot, with patience and a bit of luck, you may catch sight of a deer grazing in a clearing, a squirrel darting across the forest floor, or a porcupine foraging at the base of a pine tree. Their presence often reveals itself subtly—a rustle in the bushes, a fleeting shadow, or tracks left in the soil.

Learn to look for signs of their activity. Broken branches, claw marks on trees, scat on a game trail, or fur caught on bark tell stories of the mammals that call the forest home, even if they remain out of sight. Always take caution when interacting with wildlife. Unless you have knowledge and experience, do not approach, or engage in physical interactions with wild animals.

Trees and Vines

Look upward and take in the towering trees that define the forest. Notice how the sunlight filters through the canopy, creating a dance of light and shadow on the ground. Study the bark of a tree up close— its ridges, grooves, and colors—and see how each species has its own unique pattern. Notice how the bark of some trees curls back to reveal the inner bark or phloem. Enjoy the pattern work the woodpeckers have put into finding boring beetles within the trees.

Vines, the acrobats of the forest, twist and climb their way toward the sun, forming intricate networks. Watch how they spiral around trees or dangle from branches, adding layers of complexity to the forest's visual tapestry. Discover the networks created by the vines, and how many trees a single group of vines has entangled. Can you trace one vine from beginning to end?

Birds

Birds bring motion and life to the forest's visual landscape. Pause to observe the flash of a red cardinal darting through the trees or the subtle camouflage of a brown wren perched on a branch. Binoculars can help you spot birds in the higher canopy, where their bright plumage and fluid movements often contrast with the greenery.

Pay attention to their behaviors. Watch how they build nests, preen their feathers, or hop from branch to branch in search of food. Birds not only enhance the forest visually but also give clues about its health and vitality. You will have the best luck sitting still for a spell to see the birds become active. They are very keen on intruders, so find a soft spot, keep quiet and look up. You will see some avian action in no time flat.

By taking the time to truly see the forest—from its smallest inhabitants to its grandest trees—you will begin to appreciate the depth and beauty that surrounds you. Each element of the forest invites you to slow down, focus, and connect with the intricate patterns of life. In the next chapter, we will explore another sense—smell—and uncover the ways scent can deepen your connection to the natural world. For now, let your eyes wander and take in the wonder that unfolds when you see the forest for the trees.

Three

Stop to Smell the Redwood

The forest contains scents that tell its story—the dampness of earth after a rainstorm, the tang of pine needles crushed underfoot, and the faint sweetness of wildflowers blooming in a hidden meadow. Among the many sensory treasures nature offers, the sense of smell often transports us to memories long forgotten, calm our minds, and deepen our connection to the present moment. In this chapter, we will explore the healing power of scent in the natural world, learning how to tune into this often-overlooked sense and let it guide us toward inner peace.

Forest Air

The first scent to greet you in the forest is its air—clean, crisp, and layered with subtle hints of greenery and earth. Take a moment to breathe deeply as you step into the woods, breathing in through your nose until your chest and belly are full, and then breathe out slowly through your mouth until you have nothing left to expel. Notice how the air feels cooler and more purified than urban or indoor settings? This purity comes from the abundance of oxygen produced by trees and plants, and the absence of pollution. Let the scent of the forest air fill your lungs, grounding you and preparing your senses for what is to come. Next, you will focus on individual items within the woods.

Give Smelling Dirt a Chance

Believe it or not, one of the most unique and grounding forest scents is petrichor—the earthy aroma released when rain hits dry soil. After a rainstorm, while the forest floor is still damp, pause and inhale deeply. Notice the richness of the earth, the freshness of rainwater mingling with the soil and detritus. This scent is not just pleasant; it's a reminder of life's cycles, evoking feelings of renewal and calm. If you are feeling adventurous, gently scoop a handful of damp soil, bring it close to your nose, and let it sift slowly to the ground through your fingers. Appreciate the layers of earthy complexity it holds. Petrichor is an aroma that scent makers have attempted to capture, but nothing compares to mother nature's elixir.

Wildflowers

Though often small and scattered under the canopy of the forest, wildflowers can surprise you with their delicate yet captivating scents.

A hidden, sunny clearing within a patch of woods, or a meadow on the edge of a stand of woodland are both great areas to find an abundance of wildflowers. Spring and Summer are the best seasons to find the most colorful and fragrant varieties. Depending on the season, you might find blossoms like honeysuckle, violets, or clover releasing sweet or grassy aromas. Kneel close to a patch of wildflowers and take a moment to appreciate their fragrance. Notice how their scent can be subtle yet deeply evocative, hinting at the rich biodiversity of the forest. Take a moment to enjoy how the aromas make you feel, and what memories they may evoke for you.

Fall Leaves

Autumn transforms the forest into a palette of colors and scents. As leaves decay, they release a musky, slightly sweet aroma that defines the season. Walk through a pile of fallen leaves and take in their scent. The smell of fall leaves often evokes nostalgia and warmth, connecting you to the earth's seasonal cycles. This is a popular, well-loved scent, and the best way to enjoy it and garner the most benefit from it is in its natural environment.

Tree Bark

Tree bark might not seem like an obvious source of scent, but it holds a subtle fragrance that varies with each species. Run your fingers along the grooves of a tree trunk, then bring your hand close to your nose. You might catch a faint, woody aroma, or, in the case of trees like birch, a slightly sweet and spicy scent. Bark often absorbs the surrounding air, carrying traces of nearby flowers, moss, or rain, making it a unique sensory experience. Did you know that cinnamon comes from the bark of the Cinnamomum verum tree?

Coniferous Trees

The sharp, clean aroma of coniferous trees like pine, cedar, and fir is one of the most iconic scents in the forest. As you walk, crush a fallen pine needle between your fingers and breathe in its fragrance. Each different type of pine has its own unique scent, take your time to sample them all. The resinous scent of conifers not only invigorates the senses but also has a calming effect, and are often used in aromatherapy. Notice how the smell of conifers varies depending on the species and the time of year.

The natural world has an infinite library of scents, each one an invitation to slow down and connect. By stopping to smell the redwood and beyond, you allow yourself to be present, to embrace the forest with an open mind, generous heart, and a curious spirit. In the next chapter, we will turn our attention to the symphony of sounds that fill the woods, learning how to listen and let nature's music calm our minds and enliven our spirits.

Four

Do You Hear That?

The forest is alive with sound. From the faint rustle of leaves to the melodic calls of birds, it offers a symphony that many of us often overlook. In our busy lives, dominated by constant chatter, to-do lists, and digital noise, we rarely take the time to truly listen. In this chapter, we will explore the rich auditory landscape of the forest, learning how to tune into its sounds and appreciate the intricate layers of life it reveals.

Wind

The wind is underappreciated, and yet carries so much importance, such as foretelling a storm's arrival, or carrying seeds from one location to another. As wind moves through the forest, it plays through the leaves and branches like an instrument. Listen to its song and notice the difference between a gentle breeze whispering through the canopy and a stronger gust that sets the entire forest in motion. Hear the creaking of the branches as strong winds bend them against their will. Internalize the power of the wind as you hear entire trees groan under the strongest of wind gusts. Be certain to ensure your safety in instances of high wind warnings and stay clear of trees in cases of severe weather.

Bugs

At first glance, insects might seem silent, but their presence often creates a subtle hum that fills the air. The buzz of bees collecting nectar or the rhythmic chirp of crickets in the evening can be both calming and mesmerizing. Try sitting still near a meadow or forest clearing, where you are likely to hear a symphony of tiny wings and legs at work. Next, move next to a water feature and listen closely to the different sounds of the insects here. You may be surprised to hear insects buzz, whirr, chirp, click, sing, rattle, crackle, swish, and lisp! Listen closely and you will hear the call of one insect from one direction, and the answer from another direction.

Birds

The forest's avian inhabitants provide some of its most recognizable and enchanting sounds. Each species brings its own unique song or call, whether it's the cheerful chirping of a sparrow or the haunting hoot of an owl at dusk. To fully appreciate these melodies, find a quiet spot, close your eyes, and wait for the symphony to begin. Focus on the variety of bird calls around you—listen for rhythms, patterns, and tones. A keen listener will hear a conversation between two birds, or the mating call of a male and the corresponding answer of his potential mate. You may hear the relentless hammering of a woodpecker or the flutter of wings as a bird takes flight. As you listen, attempt to visualize the scene in your mind.

Skittering of Ground Animals

The forest floor is rarely still. If you are patient, you may hear the soft rustle of leaves or the faint sound of scurrying across the ground. Squirrels darting between trees or rabbits hopping through underbrush create subtle yet distinct noises. Mice skittering in between fields and barns, avoiding birds of prey overhead. Listen carefully, and you might even catch the crunch of twigs as a larger animal moves nearby.

Fall Leaves and Winter Snow Underfoot

It's not always the forest creating the noises, sometimes it's the guest. Walking through the forest in autumn brings its own kind of music. The crunch of leaves beneath your boots or the swish of a foot brushing through a pile of fallen foliage can be oddly satisfying. Pay attention to how the sound changes depending on the moisture levels of the leaves or the pace of your steps. These sounds, though created by you, are as much a part of the forest as the rustling of the wind.

Do not write off winter as a time to take a hike through the forest! Winter is a wonderful time to capture moments of nature's serenity. Bundle up, put on your winter boots, and listen to the crunch of the undisturbed winter snow underneath their soles. Change the speed of your pace, and place your foot down slowly. Really absorb the contrast of the crunch of the snow against the stillness of the winter woods. Take in that peace.

Moving Water

Streams, rivers, and waterfalls are among the most soothing sounds in the forest. These sounds are one of the most recorded on sound machines to help insomniacs and fussy babies sleep at night. And no wonder, the gentle babble of a brook or the rhythmic splash of water cascading over rocks can easily create a meditative mindset. If you find a water feature on your walk in the woods, take a moment to sit nearby and let its sound wash over you. Close your eyes and attempt to separate the layers of the different sounds occurring within the movement of the water. Notice how the pitch and rhythm change as the water interacts with its surroundings. Listen for the babble over and between the rocks. Keep an ear out for the "bloop!" of a frog taking a dip.

Frogs

Near ponds and streams, frogs add their voices to the forest chorus. Their croaks and trills can vary widely depending on the species and time of day. Spring and summer evenings are truly vibrant, as frogs gather to create a layered soundscape, vocalizing their most beautiful ribbits, usually in search of love. Take the time to locate these amphibian performers and appreciate their contribution to the forest's auditory tapestry.

Distant Planes, Trains, and Automobiles

Even in the heart of the forest, human-made sounds often make their way into the mix. The distant rumble of a train or the faint hum of an airplane overhead can serve as a reminder of the outside world. Instead of viewing these as intrusions, try incorporating them into your listening experience. Their contrast with natural sounds can help highlight the forest's tranquility and distance.

By tuning into the forest's sounds, you open yourself to a world of auditory wonder. Each noise, from the smallest buzz to the largest gust of wind, is a reminder of the vitality and interconnectedness of nature. In the next chapter, we will explore the sense of touch, learning how to feel the textures and elements of the forest to deepen our connection to the natural world.

Five

Feel the Elements

The forest invites us to reach out and connect with its textures, temperatures, and elements. Through the sense of touch, we can deepen our relationship with the natural world, grounding ourselves in its rhythms and sensations. From the rough grooves of tree bark to the cool flow of a stream, every texture tells a story. In this chapter, we will explore how to use touch as a tool for discovery and connection while also learning to navigate the forest with care and respect.

Soil

Soil is the foundation of the forest, rich with life and nutrients. Scoop a handful of soil and crumble it between your fingers. Notice its texture—grainy, moist, or even sandy depending on the area. Soil holds the history of the forest, composed of decayed leaves, roots, and organic matter. As you feel its weight and texture, think about the vital role it plays in sustaining the trees, plants, and creatures around you. Feel its temperature. Is it cool, a relief to the touch on a hot summer's day? Or does it feel warm and organic, as though the life of the woodland is within it at this very moment?

Moss

Soft and spongy, moss is one of the forest's gentlest textures. Moss thrives in shady, humid areas, serving as an indicator of the forest's health. Moss is vital to an ecosystem, filtering air and controlling pathogens. Gently press your fingers against a patch of moss growing on a rock or tree. Notice how it holds moisture, its surface cool and damp. By taking a moment to feel its delicate structure, you are experiencing a part of the forest that often goes unnoticed. Be cautious not to step on moss patches, as it can be delicate.

Streams

Water provides one of the most refreshing tactile experiences in the forest. Dip your hand into a cool stream and feel the way the water flows over your skin. Feel the strength of the flow of water against your hand. Internalize its power. Notice the smoothness of stones beneath the water surface, shaped by years of current and erosion. Take a moment to splash the water on your face or let it trickle through your fingers, connecting with its purity and movement. Streams not only offer sensory engagement but also provide essential nourishment for all its inhabitants. Use caution never to drink water unless you are skilled in the knowledge of its purity or water purification.

Tree Bark

The bark of a tree is like its fingerprint, unique to each species and shaped by its environment. Run your hands over the trunk of an oak and feel the deep ridges and grooves. Touch the smooth, paper-like bark of a birch and trace the lines that run horizontally around its trunk. Notice how the bark's texture changes depending on the tree's age and health. As you explore, consider the purpose of bark—how it protects the tree and offers a home to mosses, lichens, and insects. Avoid removing bark from trees you encounter, as the bark of a tree is its protective layer, as our skin is ours.

Coniferous Trees

Fir trees offer a tactile experience through their needles, resin, and pine cones. Gently run your fingers along a branch, to feel the sharp yet flexible needles. If you break a needle or lightly scratch the bark, you may release the tree's resin, which is very sticky to the touch and carries a distinct scent. This resin acts as the tree's protective mechanism, sealing wounds and warding off pests. Pine cones, with their woody, layered textures, provide another tactile wonder. Pick up a fallen cone and feel its structure, carefully running your fingers over the scales. Each pine cone is composed of many woody, rough, and sometimes sharp scales, designed to protect the seeds within.

Caution: Poison Ivy and Poison Oak

While the forest offers many wonderful textures to explore, it's essential to tread carefully. Poison ivy and poison oak are common in many wooded areas and can cause skin irritation. Learn to identify these plants by their distinctive leaves—poison ivy typically has three shiny leaflets, with the center leaflet being the largest. Poison oak is similar to poison ivy, except the leaves resemble the shape of oak leaves, and have fuzz on both sides of the leaflets. Avoid touching them directly, and if you accidentally make contact, wash the area with soap and water as soon as possible. Respecting these plants' boundaries ensures a safe and enjoyable experience in the forest.

Through touch, the forest becomes more than a visual landscape—it transforms into an experience you can connect with on a physical level. By feeling the elements, you ground yourself in the moment and form a deeper appreciation for the natural life around you. In the next chapter, we will explore the sense of taste, learning how to safely and mindfully engage with the forest's edible offerings while respecting its balance.

Six

Taste With Caution!

The forest is full of edible treasures, but venturing into the world of wild flavors requires both curiosity and caution. Nature's bounty includes nuts, berries, flowers, and more, but not everything is safe to consume. This chapter will guide you through the art of tasting the forest safely and responsibly, helping you connect with its offerings while respecting the delicate balance of the ecosystem.

Nuts

Nuts are among the forest's most accessible and rewarding edible treats. Acorns, chestnuts, and hazelnuts can often be found scattered beneath trees. However, most nuts require preparation to be palatable. Acorns, for instance, need to be leached to remove their bitterness. Always ensure you can correctly identify edible nuts, as some, like horse chestnuts, are toxic. When in doubt, consult a reliable guide or expert before consuming.

Ferns

Fiddleheads, the young, coiled fronds of certain ferns, are a seasonal delicacy in many forests. Gathered between late April to early June, they must be harvested when they are tightly curled and cooked thoroughly to eliminate any potential toxins. The flavor is often described as a cross between asparagus and spinach. Take care to identify edible fern species, such as ostrich ferns, as not all varieties are safe to eat.

Leaves

Certain leaves can provide a surprising addition to your forest-tasting experience. Young dandelion greens, sorrel, and plantain leaves are edible and packed with nutrients. Their flavors range from tart to slightly bitter, making them a unique addition to your outdoor exploration. Always pick leaves from areas free of contamination and ensure proper identification before consumption. These greens are commonly used in salads, wines, and sometimes just eaten as-is.

Flowers

Flowers are not only visually stunning but can also offer unique flavors. Wild violets, elderflowers, lavender, and dandelion blossoms are commonly edible and can add a sweet or floral note to your tasting adventure. Be mindful to harvest flowers sparingly, leaving plenty for pollinators and the ecosystem. My personal favorite floral confection is lavender cookies!

Berries

The forest offers a variety of berries, from the familiar blackberries and raspberries to the more elusive elderberries and huckleberries. Berries can be a delightful snack, but caution is essential. Some berries, such as nightshade or baneberries, are highly toxic and can be mistaken for edible varieties. Other berries need to be eaten with caution, such as elderberries, which carry multiple risks if not prepared properly. Only consume berries you can confidently identify as safe.

Mushrooms

Mushrooms are perhaps the most exciting yet dangerous forest edibles. Varieties like chanterelles, morels, and porcini are prized for their flavors, but the risk of misidentification is high. Many toxic mushrooms closely resemble edible ones. Always consult an experienced forager or mycologist and never consume a mushroom unless you are absolutely certain of its identity. Cooking mushrooms thoroughly is also essential to ensure safety.

Important Guidelines for Safe Foraging

- **Know Your Region:** The availability and safety of edible plants and fungi vary widely depending on location. Research what is safe

and common in your area.
- **Consult a Guide:** Use a reliable field guide or seek the advice of a local expert to verify the identity of anything you plan to taste.
- **Practice Moderation:** Even safe edibles can cause adverse reactions in some individuals. Start with small amounts to ensure you do not experience an allergic reaction.
- **Harvest Responsibly:** Take only what you need and avoid over-harvesting, ensuring that the forest remains abundant for wildlife and future explorers.

Tasting the forest is an extraordinary way to connect with nature, but it requires mindfulness, respect, and an abundance of caution. By approaching this activity with awareness, you can safely enjoy the edible gifts the forest has to offer. In the next chapter, we will bring everything together, reflecting on how engaging all five senses in nature can help you find balance, peace, and a renewed sense of connection to the earth.

Seven

Conclusion

As you close this book, take a moment to reflect on the journey you have embarked upon. From observing the intricate details of the forest with fresh eyes to savoring its tastes with extra care, you have explored nature through all five senses. This experience is more than just a walk in the woods; it is an opportunity to reconnect with yourself and the world around you.

By engaging your senses, you have learned to pause, appreciate, and immerse yourself in the moment. You have discovered that nature is not just the background to your life, but a living, breathing entity that can heal, inspire, and ground us. Whether it is the soothing sound of wind through the trees or the grounding touch of soil within your hands, the forest offers endless opportunities to find peace and clarity.

Now, it is your turn to take what you have learned and make it part of your life. Step away from the screens, get out of the stagnant air, find a nearby trail, and let nature guide you. Bring a friend, your fur baby, or your journal. The lessons of the forest are meant to be lived and shared.

Finally, if this book has inspired you or brought you closer to nature, I encourage you to leave a favorable review on Amazon. Your feedback not only helps others discover this book but also supports its mission of helping more people.

Thank you for walking this path with me. May your journey into the woods continue to bring you balance, peace, and a deeper connection to the earth and most importantly yourself.

Eight

Resources

Bergo, A. (2023, January 22). *Fiddlehead ferns: Identifying, harvesting and cooking*. Forager | Chef. https://foragerchef.com/how-to-identify-and-cook-fiddlehead-ferns/

Clinic, C. (2024, June 27). *Foraging 101: What to eat (and Avoid)*. Cleveland Clinic. https://health.clevelandclinic.org/foraging-101-what-to-eat-and-avoid

Collard, N. (2024, June 3). *8 poisonous berries in the United States*. Smoky Bear Ranch. https://smokybear.com/8-poisonous-berries-in-the-united-states/

Hoagland, J. (2020, June 12). *See, Hear and Touch: Communing with Nature - Princeton Perspectives*. Princeton Perspectives. https://princetonperspectives.com/see-hear-and-touch-communing-with-nature/

Lardakis, D., & Lardakis, D. (2024, September 18). *Edible mushrooms and their poisonous look-alikes.* Holden Forests & Gardens. https://hold enfg.org/blog/edible-mushrooms-and-their-poisonous-look-alikes/

Nurtured by nature. (n.d.). https://www.apa.org. https://www.apa.org/ monitor/2020/04/nurtured-nature

The Editors of Encyclopaedia Britannica. (2024, December 13). *Cinnamon | Plant, spice, History, & Uses.* Encyclopedia Britannica. https://ww w.britannica.com/plant/cinnamon

Whitbourne, K., & Bowie, D. (2023, September 14). *Petrichor: What causes the earthy smell after rain?* HowStuffWorks. https://science.hows tuffworks.com/nature/climate-weather/atmospheric/question479.ht m

www.ingramcontent.com/pod-product-compliance
Lightning Source LLC
Chambersburg PA
CBHW051402250726
48656CB00006B/2220